Shih Tzu as Pets

A Pet Guide for Shih Tzu

Shih Tzu General Info, Purchasing, Care, Cost, Keeping, Health, Supplies, Food, Breeding and More Included!

By Lolly Brown

Copyrights and Trademarks

Disclaimer and Legal Notice

Foreword

Shih Tzu breed is known for being lovely, loyal, and alert toy dog. They are great house companions especially with children. They are also known for being friendly and affectionate towards other dogs and humans. Although Shih Tzus have many positive traits, there are still more to discover about their breed.

Before you decide if you want to purchase Shih Tzu, it is best that you know the ins and outs of their breed and their characteristics. When purchasing your first Shih Tzu, there are a lot of things for you to consider. Shih Tzus are naturally lovable creature that makes great house companion. Although this holds true, some people are not fit to have this breed.

This book will discuss everything about the Shih Tzu breed; starting from its colorful history up to their everyday needs, grooming, health, and general welfare.

Table of Contents

Introduction

Shih Tzus are known to be lovable and cuddly breed of toy dogs. They are bred to become housedogs because they love to follow his humans in different rooms in the house. They make great companion for senior citizens as they love to snuggle and cuddle their owners. Another good thing about this breed, they don't need much exercise than the usual playing around the yard. Having a dog as a companion is a difficult task. Although Shih Tzus are known as being gentle, lovable, and easy to deal with. You need to make sure that you know everything about their breed.

Introduction

Being a dog owner is big responsibility. You need to take care of them properly, make sure they are healthy, safe, and happy. With all of these in mind, you need to gain the basic information up to the tiniest detail about their breed.

We will make sure that this book will give you enough information about your chosen breed. We will guide you through the process of choosing the best breed, where to buy your preferred Shih Tzu, how to raise them, how to show them off, how to reproduce, and how to take care of them when they are sick. This is your detailed journey into being a pet parent.

We will provide you with basic information, history, temperament, vaccinations, dos and don'ts, and other trivia. Also, we have links to various resources to aid you further. We hope this will be a great help in your journey. Have fun reading!

Chapter One: Basic Information

Shih Tzus are easily adaptable, dog friendly, intelligent, a great house companion, and even pup friendly! But, before you run off to purchase your first pet, you need to get to know this small and lovable creature. You need to exert time and effort to get to know them to fully know how to attend to their needs.

First essential thing that you need to know about Shih Tzus – they do not hunt, guard, or tunnel anywhere, they only do thing and they do it great, they are great house companions who likes to sit on your lap. They effortlessly stride, showing great drive, with head and tail held highly, showing that they are of ancient royal descent.

Here, you will know the biological information, as well as the origin and history of this breed. This, together with the information that you will read through the next few chapters, will equip you with necessary information to own and raise your own Shih Tzu.

The Royal History

This loyal little furball has a rich and royal Chinese history. It has flourished from being a regal pup to a lovable, gentle, and loyal house pet. This breed was believed to be a crossbreed between small Tibetan dog breeds, such as Lhasa Apsos and Pekingese.

Many people have associated the breed with Dowager Empress Tzu His, who ruled China in 1861-1908, and labeled the dogs as sacred. But, this breed has appeared as far as 2000 years ago. The breed was offered as temple dogs to Chinese emperors developed by Tibetan monks, although it is unclear when the breed has started. Also, they were believed to have carried lamas souls who had not yet reached nirvana.

Traditionally called "Shih-tzu Kou" or "Lion Dog", this breed was admired by the Imperial court due to facial features that resembles a lion which is known as the animal ridden by Buddha to go to earth.

This little breed was an exclusive property of the royal court during the Ming and Manchu dynasties. Aside from this, Shih Tzu were used as bed warmers, sometimes placed at the feet of emperors, and carried inside the robes of noble people. These little furball had disappeared after the Chinese imperial rule; fortunately, some dogs were presented to foreigners. All Shih Tzus descend from only 14 dogs. Soon enough, this breed are spread all over Europe and USA because they were given as gifts to the noble people.

Shih Tzu has become well known to the world during the 20th century when it first entered its first show ring but what first was confused with Lhasa Apso. A standard description was finally set by Madam de Breuil in 1938. During its early development, there were many descriptions and nicknames for Shih Tzus:

- Chin Chia Huang Pao – golden yellow dog
- Chin Pan To Yueh – yellow dog with white mane
- Yi Ting Mo – black dogs
- Hua Tse – multicolored dog

In the later years, it was formally introduced to the American Kennel Club when it was brought to the United States in March 1969.

Size, Life Span, and Physical Appearance

- Shih Tzus are sturdy, lively, alert, little lap dogs that weigh 9 – 16 lbs. for both male and female species and stands at 8 – 11 inches. The body length is greater than its height and is overall proportional.

- This small dog breed has a round head, double coat, and black nose. They typically have large round black colored eyes, but blur and liver dogs have light colored eyes. Their wide eyes show innocence, warmth, friendliness, and trustworthiness. A defining characteristic of the Shih Tzu is its heavy overbite. Further, their ears are pendant, high-set tail which is thickly covered by hair.

- Shih Tzu's double coat has a thick, wooly undercoat combined with long, abundant, silky topcoat. The change in coat happens between 10 to 12 months in age. They can have any color possible.

- The muzzle is short, squared, and unwrinkled, they are categorized as brachycephalic, which means their muzzles if flat.

Quick Facts

Origin: Tibet, China

Pedigree: crossbreed of Lhasa Apso and Pekingese breeds.

Breed Size: small size (toy dog)

Body Type and Appearance: Has a small yet sturdy body, pendant ears, high-set tail, curved backwards which rests on its tail. Its body is covered generously with hair.

Group: Shih Tzu Club of England, American Kennel Club, American Shih Tzu Club

Height: 11 inches or 27.94 cm

Weight: average of 9 – 16 pounds

Coat Length: dense, long, and flowing double coat

Coat Texture: soft, puffy

Color: black, white, brindle, liver, blue, liver & white, black & white, light brown, dark brown, and gold

Temperament: fierce, well-behaved, alert, vigilant, affectionate, courageous, friendly

Strangers: friendly around strangers

Other Dogs: both genders get along with other dogs

Other Pets: gets along well with other pets

Training: stubborn to train, needs to have rewards to make them follow you

Exercise Needs: daily 20 – 25 minute brisk walking

Health Conditions: generally healthy but predisposed to common illnesses such as Canine hip dysplasia, Pattelar luxation, Juvenile renal dysplasia (JRD), bladder infection, keratitis, proptosis, distichiasis, ectopia cilia, ear infection, umbilical hurnia, snuffles

Lifespan: average 11 to 14 years

Chapter Two: Shih Tzu as Pets

You are now equipped with the basic knowledge and background of this amazing and lovable lion dog. It doesn't need to stop there, before purchasing your first Shih Tzu, there are a lot of things for you to consider. Shih Tzus are naturally lovable creature that makes great house companion. Although this holds true, some people are not fit to have this breed. You should be ready with the temperament of Shih Tzus. In here, you will get a whole lot of information to make sure that this breed is suited for you. In this chapter, we will discuss Shih Tzu as a pet, how it deals with other animals, behavioral characteristics, temperament, and compatibility with other dogs and breeds, and how to purchase one legally.

What Makes It a Great Pet

Acquiring a pet is a big decision, you must know how it acts and behaves to give it the needed love and care it needs. A Shih Tzu is an excellent choice if you want a lovable housedog as a companion. Shih Tzus are proud dogs. They hold their head and tails while presenting itself. Although this might give off an arrogant vibe, but they are happy, sweet-natured, and less demanding as other toy breeds.

Shih Tzus are known as loyal and devoted dogs especially to their masters. Further, they are only a small breed which is great for apartments and small homes. They are easily adaptable, can cope up with different pets, and friendly – even with strangers. Overall, Shih Tzus don't go into much trouble even though they don't obey quickly and they will love you no matter what happens.

Temperament and Behavioral Characteristics

- They are known to be lively and outgoing toy dogs.
- They are extrovert in nature, like to cuddle and snuggle all people.
- They thirst for human connection and like to be pet.
- They constantly jump up and ready to play with its

owners and other humans.

- They are always happy when there are people around them.
- This breed is great for first time owners because they are eager to please their masters.
- They can be suspicious of strangers but wouldn't act aggressive towards them.
- They are too trusting, often jumping into people's lap.
- Some Shih Tzus suffer separation anxiety because they cling too much to their owners.
- They are great with small pets and children.
- They can handle cold and heat at the same time.
- They love to get playful with its owner and other people.
- They are amazing watch dogs.
- They are easy to adapt to various scenarios.

Behavioral Characteristics with other Pets

Shih Tzus are great with other household pets. They get along well with other dogs or animals. You just need to take precaution when introducing a Shih Tzu puppy to an older pack; it will slightly have a hard time coping, especially when it figures out who the Alpha Dog is.

Should You Choose a Shih Tzu?

In this part, we will give you reasons why or why not you need a Shih Tzu dog in your house. Take time to read through each bullet and decide if you still want to own one.

<u>Yes</u>

- A great family companion, Shih Tzus are great for singles or family with older kids.
- This breed is sweet-natured. They can be your snuggle buddy during a TV show marathon or simply have a joyous playtime with it.
- They only require short walks or an indoor play time.
- They can easily adapt to new environments. They can be introduced to new people and pets.
- Shih Tzus are peaceful with other pets
- It sheds less than other breeds.

<u>No</u>

- They can get jealous easily with babies or young children.
- Without proper training, older Shih Tzus may growl at disrespectful kids.
- They need to be brushed regularly to avoid tangled hairs.

- This breed needs a regular appointment with a groomer for trims and proper hair care.
- Somehow difficult to housebreak.
- Has several health problems due to its short face.

Legal Requirements and Dog Licensing

If you are planning to purchase a Shih Tzu as your companion, there are certain restrictions and regulations that you need to be aware of. Licensing requirements for pets varies in different countries, regions, and states. In the United States there are no federal requirements for licensing dogs or even cats – these rules are regulated at the state level. While it is true that most states do not have a mandatory requirement for people to license their dogs, it is always a good idea to do so because it will not only serve as protection for your pet but also for you.

Here are some things you need to know regarding the acquirement of Shih Tzu dogs both in United States and in Great Britain.

United States Licensing for Dogs

- There are no federal requirements for licensing dogs in the United States they are only determined at the state level.

- Licensing requirements vary from one state to another, but most states do require dog owners to register and license their dogs.

How to Obtain a License?

- You will have to provide proof that your dog has been vaccinated against rabies.

- Renew it each year along with your dog's rabies vaccination.

- Dog licenses only cost about $25 (£16.25) per year, which is not a big expense. There might be additional requirements that need to be submitted in other states. The license will be considered temporary status until all documents are received.

Even if your state or region does not require you to license your dog, it is still a good idea to do so. If your dog escapes or gets lost, having him properly identified will significantly increase the chances of you finding him. A dog license is attached to an identification number which is linked to you – if someone finds your dog; they will be able to find your contact information through the license. You can also add an ID tag to your dog's collar along with his license for good measure.

United Kingdom Licensing for Dogs

- It is mandatory for dog owners to license their dogs.

- The main difference, however, is that European dog owners do not need to vaccinate their dogs against rabies because the disease has been eradicated. Dog licenses are renewed annually and they are not a significant expense.

- In some cases you will need to get a special permit if you plan to travel with your dog into or out of the country.

Cost of Owning a Dog

Here, we will give you an insight on how much money you need to spend to purchase and take care for a Shih Tzu. This section will cover purchase fee, toys, accessories, grooming supplies, licensing, and other related needs. Taking care of a new pet is a big responsibility. You need to be prepared, not only in the mental, physical, but also in the financial aspect. Adding a new creature in your home would mean more food, treats, toys, grooming, and other basic necessities. You need to make sure that you have enough money to raise your own dog.

You need to prepare your budget for all the expenditure that you will have. It will begin in purchasing your dog, buying accessories, buying food and treats, up to the health care. This might be difficult to handle at first, but it is like a raising your own child. A scary but amazing journey you will undergo.

The overall cost for your dog-related expenses will depend on the store and availability of resources. Some stores might hike up their prices if they have limited stocks. Further, the brand and quality will determine how much you will spend and how long the item will last.

This section will help you determine if you are financially ready to own a Shih Tzu as a pet.

Price of a Shih Tzu

Shih Tzu is an adorable and lovable dog breed, because of this many people want to own and sell this breed. Further, people like to own this breed as they make great house pet that require little to moderate attention possible. Also, they make great show dogs; they can join contests to show off its beauty and skills.

The average price of a Shih Tzu is depending on its breeding. A carefully bred Shih Tzu with no medical issues will cost $700 to $1500. Some Shih Tzu puppies will cost as much as $2000 depending on the area where it is bred. Also, a breeder with quality show puppies would ask more.

You need to be careful in buying your first Shih Tzu puppy; some puppies are priced high even though they are not of quality bred. You must look into the medical records and the pup's parent before you purchase it. Further, buying from a trusted friend will cost less, while a trusted pet store could give you a higher quality pup.

Other Essentials

Buying your puppy is not the only expense that you will have if you plan to own one. You need to keep in mind additional expenses such as vaccinations, bed, vet consultations, toys, and etc.

Be financially prepared with all these things. You might not see that they are essential at first, but these will come handy. These are essential things that will make taking care of shih tzu a breeze, further, this will make them more comfortable in their living.

Bed ($10-$50)

Shih Tzus are only a small breed of dog, you could buy a small to a normal-sized bed and it will last for a long time.

Look for a great dog bed as Shih Tzus are susceptible to hip dysplasia, they need soft and comfortable mattresses for maximum back support.

It is still best to buy your beds on a physical shop, as you can touch the mattress and see if it fits the needs for your dog. Further, you can choose from different available designs and structures. Make sure you choose the best bed that would best fit the personality of your pup.

Toys ($20-$100)

There is lot of toys your Shih Tzu could choose from. You need to find the best suited toy for your dear pet. You have a lot to choose from, from balls, squeaky toys, bone toys, and etc. This will provide a variety of activities for your dog so it would not be bored easily. Maximize the use of toys as a way for them to learn words and tricks. Also, teach your pup ways on how to utilize his toys efficiently. But, don't buy too many toys as it may not use it and you will just end up with garbage.

Also, make sure that you have a box where your dog could put all its toys away. This will ensure that you can keep account of all the toys and your house wouldn't have toys lying around anywhere.

Grooming Tools ($100-$500)

Shih Tzus require a lot of grooming tools. They have double coats, which needs to be brushed daily or just regularly to be maintained. Some brushes that you need are: face comb, two level comb, de-matting comb for the face, and a body comb. Aside from that, you need to buy a spritzer to keep the coat shiny and healthy. The spritzer will also serve as a sunscreen protection during summer.

There are a lot tools to choose from, it is best to consult this book, your vet, and your groomer about the necessary tools for your pups. You need to buy these things as they are necessary to emergencies at home.

Further, owning these tools will help you practice grooming the dog yourself. Self-grooming will ensure that you will give the best possible cut for your dog, further; it will give you from financial responsibilities it may add on.

Dog Food and Treats ($50-100)

A key to keeping your dog happy is giving it healthy dog food and treats. Dog foods have special nutrients that will help your dog to grow and have strong bones. Further, dog treats are not just used as a dessert; you can use these to train your dogs to follow your commands.

Dog foods are essential to your dog's health. This is the key for your dog to have the best nutrients in its body.

Make sure you read through the package and its nutritional value.

Medical Expenses

There are several medical expenses that you will encounter when you purchase a pet, some include micro-chipping, spay/neuter surgery, vet consultation, and vaccinations. Although these are only incidental expenses, you need to save for a rainy day because you don't know when you might need to rush your pup to the hospital.

Micro-chipping

Micro-chipping is not required by the United States and United Kingdom government, but it is an essential step if you want to keep your dog safe. Your dog could play around and might go out on open doors or windows if unsupervised.

Your dog might be taken into a shelter if found wandering on the street, a microchip would help identify your dog. Micro-chipping is a process where a chip is implanted under your dog's skin which carries information about the owner. It is a painless procedure that only costs $50, but could go higher for some states.

Initial Vaccinations

Initial vaccinations are needed if you have purchased/gotten your Shih Tzu at a young age. Puppies are prone to common viral infections, it is best to have initial vaccines and boosters as soon as they are ready. Although mothers could give the essential antibodies at the early stage, vaccines are still important as they provide long time benefits for your pup. Giving puppy's vaccines, at an early age, could definitely lengthen their life. The price of vaccines may start at $50.

Spay/Neuter Surgery

Spay/neuter surgery is one of the hardest decision you need to do for your dogs.

If you don't plan to breed Shih Tzu or don't have the time to take care of more puppies, this track might be for you.There are also some benefits when you spay/neuter your pet. First, spaying/neutering will lessen the chance of uterine infections, breast cancer, and testicular cancer. Also, spaying/neutering will eliminate unwanted puppies from your house. Further, you male dog won't roam around and find a mate, since it can't go into heat.

The price for this surgery depends on the gender of your dog and where you will have it done.

Veterinary Consultations

Veterinary consultation is a must for pets. You must keep your vet updated with the condition of your pet to keep it healthy. Your Shih Tzu should have a regular check up every six months. You might need to go to the vet more often when it is less than a year old, especially when it is being vaccinated. Average cost per veterinary visit is about $40. You need to create a rainy day fund for your pet for veterinary consultation and medicine.

Chapter Three: Purchasing a Shih Tzu

You have now the essential knowledge about legally owning and maintaining your Shih Tzu. You, now, have considered its pros and cons. The next step is finding the best way to purchase your chosen breed. There are several ways to purchase your breed; you need to find the best way possible to ensure that you get the best value for your money while maintaining integrity for your chosen breed.

In this chapter, we will give you valuable information about finding the best Shih Tzu breeder, how to select the best breeder, and get the healthiest puppy. Further, we will give you tips for puppy-proofing your home and ways to welcome your new Shih Tzu puppy.

Where to Purchase your Shih Tzu

There are a lot of places where you can purchase your first puppy, here; we will give you the pros and cons of each choice. Keep an open mind and compare each choice to figure out which place suits you the best.

Purchasing your first dog is a difficult task; it requires extensive research and a whole lot of effort. It is difficult to find a great breeder who will divulge extensive knowledge for your pup's history that would sell it at a small price.

You may need to call up a few people or places to find the best puppy, although the find might be exhausting – if you have found the best pup, it will all be worth it.

Local Pet Stores

Local pet stores are the first choice of many people when buying pets. They are easily accessible to many houses. Also, you can have your pup delivered easily at home if you're near them. Shih Tzus are a popular breed; you can find them easily at any pet store within your area. However, pet shops won't disclose you the breed and how the puppies and parents were raised. Pet stores employees don't have an idea where they get their pets. Further, some pet stores don't take good care of the dogs that they raise. Be careful in choosing this option.

This path might be for those who have little to no time in finding the perfect dog. You just go to your local pet shop and buy off the available dog there. But, if you plan to have the best pup with the best value, this path is not for you. You need to have patience and determination to find the best that would fit for you.

Private Breeders

One of the best choices in purchasing your first pup is through backyard/private breeders. A referral from a family or friend constitutes greatly to your decision. You can get to know the breeder, the pups, and the parents easily. This will let you determine if the pup has been taken care from the beginning. Further, you can bargain for a lower price, and they might even tell you some tips on how to take care of your pup.

A disadvantage from this option is that you need to come to the house/place personally to visit and inspect the puppies. Also, you need to be the one to pick up the pup to take it home. Further, it might take up time and money before purchasing your dream pup because you need to find a great breeder.

This path is best for sociable people who want to meet new breeders. This could lead to new breeders for possible breeding of the dogs, resulting to a profitable business and new friendship, but this path is not for those who does not have time to talk to people and investigate on their background.

Online Pet Shops/ Online Private Breeders

Since the era of the internet has flourished, the online world has given many opportunities for online sellers. This will be a great option if you are a busy person; you can just look it up online and meet up for the purchase. You can join online forums to know which sites would give you the best breed possible. However, you won't have the opportunity to critique how the pup was bred, its health, and its parent. You need to keep a keen eye on its physical characteristics before buying it.

Choosing this path may be scary at first, there are a lot of things that you need to know before buying off from online sellers. First, you need to be alert for possible scamming situations. Make sure that the breeder has a reputable background and has previous experience with other people.

Further, you need to make sure that they will provide with necessary information about the puppy and the parents. Sellers who keep this information a secret is not trustworthy, their pups might not be that healthy or the parents that have health problems.

Tips in Choosing a Reputable Breeder

We have given you a lot of options on where to buy your Shih Tzu. You also need to do extensive research on where to buy your chosen breed. Compiling their pros and cons will let you decide where you can buy the best pup.

You don't want to end up with an unhealthy puppy that you will take care for 10-15 years. Have an extensive research before buying your puppy; make sure to take note of everything before you make this big purchase.

Make sure to list down every little detail from different breeders so that you will not regret the decision that you will make for you and your furry pet.

Here, we will give you tips in finding the best Shih Tzu breeder:

Tip#1: Ask your friends, family, and relatives if they know a respectable breeder.

Tip#2: Join online forums and talk to other dog owners and ask for opinions where to find reputable breeders.

Tip#3: Research websites about Shih Tzus, some sites link to breeders that they like.

Tip#4: Make sure these websites are real and have reputable background, check signs for bogusness, if you see a little red flag, back out now.

Tip#5: If the website doesn't provide any information about the facilities or the breeder, you shouldn't waste your time with them.

Tip#6: Contact each breeder individually. Ask them of their knowledge and experience in breeding Shih Tzu.

Tip#7: Remove breeders who don't answer your questions truthfully and honestly, this will enable you if the breeders are actually reputable or just hobby breeders.

Tip#8: Expect a reputable breeder to ask you questions about yourself as well. A responsible breeder wants to make sure that his pups go to good homes.

Tip#9: Make sure you allot time to go through every detail, although tedious, will give you amazing results.

Tip#10: Schedule visits from your selected breeders; ask for a tour on their facilities.

Tip#11: Narrow down, again, your choices. Remove those with unorganized and dirty facilities – you don't know if your future pup has been bred in this.

Tip#12: If you still can't decide, go back to square one and list down every detail possible. Once you are settled, place reservation deposit for your chosen pup.

What to Look For in a Shih Tzu?

After you have determined where you will buy, who to buy from, you get to know your future pup. Since you already know that your chosen is reputable and reputable, you need to critique the Shih Tzu, not only physically, but also behaviorally, and mentally. You need to allot time to get to know the puppy, make sure that the characteristics and behavior fits your personality. Having a dog that would contrast what you believe in is a difficult task.

Just a reminder, you shouldn't take in puppy home if it is younger than 8 weeks. Some states prohibit selling a puppy less than 8 weeks of age. You need to make sure that the puppy is fully weaned and is eating solid food. If the breeder has not divulged this information, observe the puppy/ies for several days, so you can know if they are ready to be own their own.

This section will give you the characteristics of a healthy pup. We have extensively researched all the best qualities for a Shih Tzu. Check off those that apply to the dog that you wanted to purchase.

Check the Pup's Physical Characteristics

- Examine the pup's body thoroughly for any signs of illness and potential injuries.
- The pup/s stomach shouldn't be distended or swollen.
- The pup/s stomach should be able to walk and run normally without any mobility problems.
- Check the coat color and skin.
- The pup/s ears should be clean, and clear with no discharge or inflammation.
- The pup/s should have clear, bright eyes with no brownish discharge.
- Make sure that its teeth and gums are also in good condition
- Avoid any pups that look lethargic and those that have difficulty moving because they could be sick.

Check the Pup's Behavior

- The pup/s should be active, and playful, interacting with each other in a healthy way.
- Try to observe the litter as a whole, and watch how the pups interact with each other so you can determine their personalities.

- Play with the pup individually so you can determine its individual traits – so you can choose the best for you.
- Try picking them up to see if they are frightened to human contact or not, if they are too scared, it could mean that they are not properly socialized.
- If all the pups are in good condition, and seems to like you, that's a good sign that your breeder is also reputable. All you have to do now is to choose who best connects with you.

List of Breeders and Rescue Websites

There are many ways to choose the breeder in your area; you need to do several extensive researches before you decide which breeder you want to buy from. Buying without researching is a mortal sin, because you might end up with an unhealthy puppy that won't live for a long time. It is not just a waste of money, but also a waste of effort, love, and dog's life.

If you have chosen where to buy your pup, you might still keep an open mind in buying an adult dog. There are many abandoned Shih Tzu adult dogs available in shelters that are looking for new homes. When you adopt an adult dog, you are saving a life. Although it might be difficult raising an already adult Shih Tzu, they can show more love and affection than the baby Shih Tzus. These rescued adult Shih Tzus are sometimes already trained and are easy to pick up basic commands.

Adopting an adult dog is much cheaper, and some might even give away free cages and accessories. Also, some dogs are already house trained, spayed or neutered, and even vaccine. Here is the list of breeders and adoption rescue websites around United States and United Kingdom:

United States Breeders and Rescue Websites

Shih Tzu Rescue
<https://www.shihtzurescue.org>

SASS Rescue
<http://www.sassrescue.com/>

STRMN Shih Tzu Rescue of Minnesota
<https://www.shihtzuerescuemn,org>

STFBR
<http://www.stfbr.org>

New Beginnings Shih Tzu Rescue, Inc.
<http://www.nbstr.org>

Tzu Zoo Rescue

<http://www.tzuzoorescue.com>

National Mill Dog Rescue

<https://www.milldogrescue.org>

Save a Rescue

<http://www.savearescue.org>

Bluegrass Shih-Tzu Rescue

<http://www.shihtzurescueky.org>

Ohio Fuzzy Pawz

<http://www.ohiofuzzypawz.com>

Peke A Tzu Rescue

<http://www.pekeatzurescue.com >

Shih Tzu Rescue of Central WI

<http://www.shihtzurescueofcentralwi.org/>

Shih Tzu Garden

< http://www.shihtzugarden.com/>

Puppies in a Box Shih Tzu

< http://www.puppiesinabox.com/>

High Point Shih Tzu

< http://www.highpointshihtzu.com/>

United Kingdom Breeders and Rescue Websites

Southern Shih Tzu Rescue UK

<https://www.southernshihtzurescue.org.uk>

Shih Tzu Club

<http://www.theshihtzuclub.co.uk>

Shih Tzu Dogs | Pets4Homes

<http://www.pets4homes.co.uk/>

Shih Tzu Breed Rescue

 <http://www.thekennelclub.org.uk/>

UK Rescue Dogs

<http://www.rescuedogs.org.uk/breed/shih-tzu/>

Dogs Trust

< https://www.dogstrust.org.uk/rehoming/ >

Many Tears Animal Rescue

< www.manytearsrescue.org/>

Lone Star Shih Tzu & Lhasa Apso Rescue

Protecting Your New Pet

Having new puppies at home will cause you some serious trouble if you don't train it as soon as possible. Here are some tips on how to prepare your home for your new found pet:

- Place all of your food in tightly lidded containers and store them in the cupboard or pantry.

- Store all of your medications (prescription and over-the-counter) safely in a medicine cabinet.

- Remove any toxic houseplants from your home or move your plants so they are well out of your puppy's reach.

- Check to make sure none of the plants on your property are toxic to dogs – if they are, remove them or fence them off so your puppy can't get into them.

- Cover any open bodies of water that could pose a drowning hazard for your puppy – this includes toilets, sinks, ponds, pools, and more.

- Make sure all of the outlets in your home are protected by plastic covers.

- Tie up the cords for your blinds as well as electric cords so your puppy can't chew on them.

- Keep all of your cleaning supplies stored away where your puppy can't get into them – this includes supplies kept in the garage.

- Pick up small objects from the floor and put them away – this includes things like toys, rubber bands, pieces of string, etc.

- Keep your puppy in a confined space at first. This will enable you to train it easily and will learn commands easily.

- You need to have toys and chew toys while you are away. Some pups might misbehave when you are not around, to prevent this from happening, they should have leisure activities in their area.

- Hide trash cans and bins that are easily accessible by these dogs. They might easily climb this up, pick up the trash, and eat the spoiled or rotten foods.

- Secure all your appliances; make sure that those won't be easily knocked down because puppies and dogs love to run around the living room.

These are just some ways for you to puppy proof your home. This will ensure that your puppy will be safe and your home will be safe. These might not be an easy task to fix, a task that will require you to modify your living space, but these will greatly help you to raise your puppy – especially when you are alone. After knowing these things, look around your house and see what things are dangerous for your pup.

Chapter Four: Taking Care of Your Shih Tzu

Shih Tzus are great home companions, these dogs can easily adapt to new environment and new living conditions.

Taking care of a Shih Tzu is not an easy task. You need to know the ins and outs, starting from how it will live, the vet requirements, exercise needs, supplements, and many more. Raising a Shih Tzu is just like raising your own child, you should take care starting from its first steps until its last breathe. In this chapter, we will provide you with new information on how to give a happy and healthy life for your pup. Also, we will give you tips on its needed housing requirements, crate set-up and providing the best exercise possible.

Housing Requirements

Shih Tzus are just little dog breeds. They can live in small apartments or in big houses, but make sure they have enough room to roam around. Although Shih Tzus are little creatures, they still need to be walked around the yard or a block to maintain its weight. It is not ideal for Shih Tzu to gain extra weight. Below are some required items you need for your dog:

- ➤ Bed or Crate
- ➤ Blanket
- ➤ Food and water dishes
- ➤ Toys
- ➤ Collar, leash, and harness
- ➤ Grooming supplies

These are just some of the requirements that you need to take care of your beloved fur ball. It might cost a lot at first, but these will be for the long run and they will benefit you and your pup for a long time.

Bed or Crate

Earlier, we mentioned that you can buy a small dog bed for your Shih Tzu, but, don't let that hinder you to buy a bigger bed. Buying a bigger bed means giving your dog bigger space to move and sleep on. You can add disposal pillows and bed sheets to make it more comfortable for your Shih Tzu. Disposal pillows are ideal because puppies like to bite and play with them and soon will destroy them.

Based on some interviews, new puppies like to sleep on a place where they would feel safe. This is a normal attitude as they may still be adjusting to a new environment, so don't force them to sleep on their designated place yet.

It is totally your decision if you want to buy a cage for your Shih Tzu. Caging your Shih Tzu might be a bad idea. The dog might not be as affectionate as you want to be. Further, they might not like staying at a cage because they like to play and cuddle with their humans.

Food/Water Dishes

Food and water bowls are essential to your pet. It comes in all shapes and sizes but you need to find the one that suits best your dog.

Shih Tzus are relatively small breeds, they can use small to medium sized bowls. It is best to buy stainless steel and ceramic bowl because they don't gather much bacteria unlike plastic. These food and water bowls will be used for a long time, so you need to buy sturdy materials that would not bulge when it plays with the bowls.

Toys

Shih Tzus are playful creature. Make sure they have enough toys hanging around so they can be occupied and won't chew on your furniture.

There are a lot of toys available on the market; you need to utilize these things as they can be both beneficial and harmful for your dogs. It is beneficial because you can use this for housetraining and commands, they can learn easily through rewards and treats. However, if your dog has too many toys, it might get confused and not follow you anymore. You need to prioritize and choose the best possible toy for your beloved fur ball.

Collar, Leash and Harness

Buying a collar for your Shih Tzu is important. Collars are used to attach your dog's license and tags. Make sure that the collar is just about the right size, it should not be too loose or too tight for it. A leash in an important accessory to buy for your dog, it gives you the chance to walk your Shih Tzu with ease.

A harness is also a good investment. It is used as a controller for your dog's movement when you are walking or running with it. Further, it would put off pressure on your dog's neck and throat. Also, these things are used when you are walking your dog. You will have an easy time walking them around; also, this will provide them the exercise that they need every day – which can also exercise you.

Grooming Supplies

Shih Tzus have double coat that needs to be constantly brushed and taken care of. You need to buy grooming supplies as it lessens the cost rather than going to the groomer every time its hair is growing. Simple clipping and trimming is the key in keeping your pup's hair as fabulous as possible.

In order to keep your Shih Tzu's skin and coat in good health you'll need to brush and comb him several times a week. Have a wire pin brush on hand as well as wide-toothed comb. You may also want to buy an undercoat rake to help remove dead hairs from your Shih Tzu's coat before he sheds them all over your furniture.

Later on in this book, you can find more information on how to properly groom your pet!

Housing Temperature

You, also, need to keep in mind your house temperature. Make sure your house/apartment is in normal temperature. Shih Tzus have double coats so they tend to feel hot more than the usual.

House with hot temperatures may not be suitable for your Shih Tzu. They might often get dehydrated and may have illnesses or even die. You need to maintain the heat at its best so your dog can have a good time in your house and will be raised properly and healthy.

Guidelines on How to Keep Your Pup Happy and Safe

It is best to prepare your home before your pet arrives. 'Puppy-proofing' your home will result to protecting your puppy from various hazards and avoiding unwanted accidents. Here, we will provide you with several guidelines in keeping your puppy happy and safe:

- Install fences, a screened porch or a safe enclosure.

- Make sure that poisonous plants are out of reach for your puppies.

- Do not leave your appliances plugged, as mentioned earlier, they will chew anything including electric wires, not only is this potentially fatal for your pup but also a dangerous threat for your home.

- Train your dog to always be on leash when walking around the neighborhood.

- Make sure to keep lots of pup toys out and put anything precious and destructible away.

- Make sure to keep away toxic liquids or materials like cleaning supplies or other household items that can harm them.

- Make sure that your pup/pup will not be able to enter bathrooms or kitchens alone because it can be dangerous for them. Always supervise and keep an eye on them or better yet lock the doors so that they can't easily enter.

Chapter Five: Nutrition and Feeding

Proper nutrition is a vital key to make your puppy healthy. Feeding your Shih Tzu might not be an easy task as they easily get used to eating the dog food and might not eat anymore. Feeding your puppy will vary from their taste, age, and monetary budget. They need to have a balanced diet to ensure good health. Buying from a grocery store without researching could result to a disaster; you might know that your dog does not like the food that you will be serving it. Further, some manufacturers might not give the correct information for your puppy and might not really be good for your growing pup.

In this chapter, we will provide you with health information, nutritional needs and restrictions, feeding tips and foods that are good and harmful for your Shih Tzu. Make sure that you list down everything and make sure that you keep these in mind in your decision.

The Nutritional Needs of Dogs

To maintain your dog's health and growth, you need to give importance to its balanced diet. You need to take care in looking for the best quality of dog food to take care of its nutritional needs, vet instructions, and special needs.

Dogs have different nutritional requirements, you should need to know and utilize them fully. Just like humans, dogs need nutrients to live healthy. Make sure you keep this in mind especially when you are buying pet foods, treats, and vitamins. Here are the six important nutrients your dogs need to have a healthy lifestyle:

Minerals

Minerals can't be made by the animals, so, you should be the one to introduce it to its diet. Minerals are important because it strengthens the bones and teeth, and balances metabolism. The most important minerals for dogs include copper, calcium, phosphorus, potassium, sodium, and iron.

Water

Just like humans, water makes up 60%-70% of adult pet's body weight. Although some pet food have a small percentage of moisture, 10%, while canned food has 78% moisture. A decrease in body water can cause serious illnesses, or worse, death. Dogs need to have an accessible water bowl for their needs. Dogs like to constantly walk, run, and play around your house, having a bowl will help hydrate them easily.

Protein

Proteins are the basic building blocks of cells. Further, it is an important component in our tissues, organs, enzymes, hormones, and antibodies. Shih Tzus need this nutrient because proteins help in one's growth, maintenance, reproduction, and repair. Some good sources of protein are chicken, lamb, beef, fish, eggs, while vegetables contain only a few.

Carbohydrate

For humans, carbohydrates are essential because it provides energy, helps the intestine, and reproduction. For dogs, there is no requirement of how much diet your four-legged creature need, but there is a requirement for its glucose content. A good source of carbohydrates is brown rice and oatmeal, which is very digestive for dogs. Also, avoid soy and corn because they provide low-quality carbohydrates and of little nutritional value.

Vitamins

Just like humans, vitamins are needed for metabolism. However, dogs can't produce their own vitamins so you need to be the one to introduce vitamins in their diet.

Although they need vitamins, it is unnecessary to give them supplements unless directed by a veterinarian, your dog could be poisoned if you give them more than enough vitamins. The most important vitamins for dogs are vitamin D, vitamin A, vitamin C and vitamin E.

Fats

For pets, fats are the most concentrated source of energy; it gives your pets plenty of energy than proteins or carbohydrates. You should make sure your Shih Tzu gets a balance of omega-3 and omega-6 fatty acids to ensure proper skin and coat health. Further, fats provide insulation and protection for organic. A deficiency of fats could result to illnesses and skin problems.

Like protein, fats should come from animal-based sources like chicken fat and fish oil instead of plant-based sources like flaxseed or canola oil

How to Select a Healthy Dog Food Brand

Feeding your puppy is a difficult task, as a pet parent, you need to give the perfect dog food that would suit its need. You need to find a dog food that your pup will enjoy while maintaining within your budget. You need to remember that the dog food shouldn't upset his stomach, gives your dog plenty of nutrients, to be the healthy pup you want it to be.

We will give you a rundown of the best suggested healthy dog food brand for your furry friend:

Royal Canin Shih Tzu Dog Food- ☆ ☆ ☆ ☆ ☆

This dog food has been specifically developed to cater to your Shih Tzu's needs. This food has kibbles that make it easy for your Shih Tzu to eat, especially because pups have big tongues, and it helps to keep the dog's teeth clean.

EUKANUBA - ☆ ☆ ☆ ☆ ☆

This dog food is a runner up as the best dog food for your Shih Tzu. Although specifically designed for a Yorkshire Terrier, it still meets the nutritional and dental needs of your Shih Tzu.

Wellness CORE Natural Grain Free Dry Dog Food - ☆ ☆ ☆ ☆

This dog food is specifically designed for small breed, so you can make sure that they will love it. It is grain free that has balanced everyday nutrition for your beloved pup. Further, this feed is rich protein made from turkey and chicken. Also, this is packed with calories so you can be assured that your Shih Tzu has high energy levels. This contains natural ingredients that would guarantee safety and freshness especially for dogs with allergic reactions.

Here are some tips to choose the best dog food brand for your pup:

Get to know your dog

Your dog's physical characteristics are an important consideration in choosing the food you will give it. The amount of food you will give your pup will help avoid issues, such as obesity.

Puppies and mother need more calories as they need more energy due to high activity. Older dogs need fewer calories because they don't move much. Active dogs need more food than lap dogs. You need to know these things to give your dog the best food possible.

Read the food packaging

Understanding the food packaging will determine how much nutrients it contains. Remember that water is always a part of the dog food and might lower down the nutrients on it.

Some brands might say that their food contains "beef" or "chicken" in them; the water content could lower the nutrients up to 20%. Dinner dog foods only contain 25% of the protein it needs. Cheese-based dog food would only contain 3% of the actual nutrient.

Learn the Ingredients

Reading the ingredients could help you choose the best dog food for your dog.

Choose the brand which lists meat first because it contains the highest water content for it. Further, don't introduce a new diet to your dog, such as vegan or vegetarian, as your dogs are naturally omnivores and they might get bad reactions from it. There are many sources of meat such as skeletal muscle, tissues from the heart, esophagus, and other.

Should you switch it up?

If you think your dog has some problems with the food, it is best to consult your veterinarian first. Switching their diet to grains is not really a bad idea, but, it has a higher price point so you need to be prepared.

Don't switch up to a new diet just because a new fad comes along, such as gluten-free, consider their needs too.

Know the nutritional adequacy

Although your dog food states "complete and balanced nutrition", it is still to scrutinize the can or bad thoroughly.

A good way to know the nutritional adequacy is looking at the Association of American Feed Control Officials (AAFCO)'s standard. Membership to AAFO is only voluntarily, but they have set a high nutritional standard and they provide it to their customers.

Research and list down the pros and cons

You need to have a thorough research to find the best dog food for your puppy. Research on the manufacturers, quality control, and sourcing of ingredients. If you are still hesitant to buy the dog food, list the pros and cons to make sure you get the best value possible.

Tips for Feeding Your Pet

Feeding your pet could be a difficult task; you may not know how much is too much for it. Shih Tzus are relatively small breed so they don't need much food, or else, they'll be obese and they have a hard time losing that excess weight. You can start off by feeding your dog through the recommendation in the food package. Watch the weight and you'll see if it's enough and maintain the food. But, if there is a decline in weight, add a little more. Or, if your dog gains a lot of weight, decrease the portion. Further, determine the number of times you need to feed your pup.

When it is a puppy, you can feed your Shih Tzu freely. But, remember to switch it up to adult food and adjust the food intake. Make sure you watch the weight gain and when it reaches the 80% potential, control the portion that you will give it. Feeding your puppy is a good way to bond, make sure you prepare healthy meals for it so it can feel that you love it very much.

Chapter Six: Grooming Your Shih Tzu

Shih Tzus have double coats that need to be maintained and brushed frequently. Grooming your dog doesn't not only entail bathing, but also improving and maintaining the skin's condition. It may seem as a difficult task, but you just need to develop the habit to take a day off and spend with your pet.

In this section, we will help you to know the basics of grooming, including brushing, bathing, as well as trimming nails, cleaning his ears, and brushing its teeth. Take note of these things as they are important to keeping your puppy happy.

Grooming 101

Owning a Shih Tzu entails brushing and washing your pup often. You need to give time and effort to groom your Shih Tzu. Further, you can play around hair styles to ensure that your Shih Tzu will look very pretty. There are questions for you to consider if you want to do the grooming by yourself or hiring a professional groomer:

1. Could I groom my Shih Tzu frequently?
2. Could I afford to go to a groomer once every two months?
3. What style would I settle for my Shih Tzu?

These are some pretty difficult decisions you have to make, we are here to help you decide whether to hire a groomer or not.

Hiring a Professional Groomer

Hiring a professional groomer is an easy way to take for your dog. You can set up an appointment every six to eight weeks.

You will be left with little grooming tasks such as brushing and combing every now and then. Further, you might need to clip down the nails, brush the teeth, or something along the line.

These are some of the things your groomers do for your dog:

- Bath
- Removing mat
- Check anal glands
- Spritz cologne
- Clean ears
- Cut dog's hair
- Clip nails

However, you also need to consider these things if you still want to pursue hiring a groomer. First, you need to set a budget for the additional cost. Next, you need to have enough time to go, wait, and return to your home after every appointment. Finally, dogs don't typically like long car rides, you need to train your dogs for this circumstance.

If you plan to do it by yourself, it has advantages which you will really like. First, it only costs a little after you have purchased the materials. Plus, it gives you a chance to bond with your fur buddy. Also, it gives you the control on what you the outcome for your dog and the time you spend for it.

However, there are also disadvantages when you do-it-by-yourself. First, you need to be trained to cut your dog's hair correctly; next, you need to buy the supplies before cutting its hair. Finally, you need to establish a routine for your pup.

This path is recommended for those who don't have much time in doing it your own. Or, to those who does not to try cutting the dog's hair.

It might be scary at first but it is a bonding session, in which if you have developed the necessary skill – you might even set up a little grooming station around your area.

Recommended Tools for Grooming

If you still wish to pursue grooming your own pup, you need to be ready the following supplies. Make sure you have these things in your home so you will be ready to groom it. Here is a list of several recommended grooming tools and supplies below:

- Tote bag (for storage)
- **For puppies**
  - Puppy pin brush
  - Puppy comb

- **For adults**
  - Pin brush
  - Slicker brush
  - Bristle brush
  - Flea comb
  - Rat tail comb

- Straight shears
- Curve shears
- Thinning or blending scissors
- Blunt tipped scissors
- Dematting combs
- Blow dryer
- Shampoo and conditioner
- Nail clippers
- Dog-friendly ear cleaning solution
- Dog toothbrush
- Dog-friendly toothpaste

Some of these materials have dual purpose, you need to do further research on which brushes work the same so you'll cut some costs. Having these stuff ready could help you in any disaster, you can snip up tangles easily as to avoid a bigger mess. If you have bought the necessary materials already, you re now ready to groom your dog. Buy these from your trusted store you can have the best quality of tools available in the market.

Tips for Bathing and Grooming Shih Tzu

Now, you already have an idea of the supplies that you would need to groom your Shih Tzu. You can now groom the Shih Tzu by yourself.

First of all, you would need to prepare all the materials. Puppies are easily distracted and can get out the sink easily if you haven't prepared all the things already. Make sure all the necessary items are accessible. Train your puppies that they need to always take a bath. You can give it treats as a reward after every bath. This will ensure that you will have a breeze when you are taking care of them.

o   When you have already set up all the necessary things, you are now ready to bathe your Shih Tzu. First, you need to brush its coat before the bath. Make sure to separate the hairs and remove the tangles. Carefully brush the fur to avoid hurting your beloved pet. If you brush it too hard, they might not like bath time or even just brushing.

o   Next, you put small pieces of cotton balls into your pup's ear. This will prevent the water from entering its ear, but take caution in putting cotton as they might get stuck if it goes very deep.

- o Put your Shih Tzu on a sink with a non-slip mat. It is okay if he stands on the side of the sink, it will take time for the pup to stand on a non-slip mat. You need to lead your pup on where and how to stand when you bathe them. Training is the key when bathing your dog.

- o Wet its body thoroughly, you can do this task by spraying with a nozzle or using a small cup. After you have wet it, read the label for the shampoo. Some shampoo needs to be watered down, if not, you can proceed to massaging the pup with the shampoo. Make sure to scrub every part of the dogs' body for three to five minutes. Also, look for flakes or fleas in its body. This is a good time to inspect if there are suspicious bumps around the area.

- o Get a washcloth and dip into sudsy water. You will use this to wash the dog's face. Take care not to make contact with its eye. Further, you can remove tear stains using a small-bristled brush.

- o Make sure to rinse the pup thoroughly and apply conditioner to protect and enhance its coat. Leaving suds on your pup will result to flakes, and sometimes, infections.

Groom Some More!

Aside from the abovementioned tasks, there are also other things you need to do to fully groom your dog. Keep this in mind to maintain the cleanliness and health of your pup. These other tasks are just tedious as the first one, but these will help promote hygienic health for your pup.

Brushing Your Pet's Teeth

We might not get a hang of brushing our dog's teeth, but it is actually an important part of the grooming process. Oral diseases are very common among pets and can lead to further problems. Here are some simple tips on how to brush your dog's teeth and mouth:

- o Place a small amount of dog-friendly toothpaste on its toothbrush.
- o Brush its teeth, then move to different spots until he gets used to it.
- o Be sure to reward your dog after brushing his teeth so he learns that good behavior earns him a treat. This will make things much easier for you in the long run.

Cleaning Your Shih Tzu's Ears

Ears can easily breed bacteria if you don't keep them clean that may lead to ear infections if not treated properly. With this in mind, you should always clean your dog's ear to keep it hygienic. Here are some simple tips on how to brush your dog's teeth and mouth:

- o Clean your dog's ears
- o add a few drops of a dog-safe ear cleaning solution to the ear canal
- o Massage the outside the ears by hand to spread the solution.
- o Use clean cotton balls to clean away any buildup inside your dog's ears.
- o Let your dog's ears dry.

Trimming Your Dog's Nail

- o Trimming your dog's nail may scare you at first. But, it is time to stop bringing your dog to the vet or groomer to have its nail trimmed.

- o Clipping dog's nails needs to be done every two months. Make your pup feel comfortable by through training it from the very beginning.

o Also, some dogs resist nail clipping, it is best to clip its nails when it is tired and right before sleeping.

o If you still plan to clip its nail, make sure to look for the vein before clipping. This vein is quite crucial because it might cause bleeding and blood clotting.

Chapter Seven: Showing Your Shih Tzu

Shih Tzus are wonderful creatures and they are a good breed to show in different exhibitions. They are well-mannered but can be a bit stubborn when training. In order to show your Shih Tzu, however, you have to make sure that he meets the requirements for the breed standard and you need to learn the basics about showing dogs. Showing your Shih Tzu would mean great honor and reward money to spend to your puppy. Also, Shih Tzus hold their head and tail high, they are meant to be shown off to people and other dogs.

In this chapter, you will get information about the standard breed for Shih Tzus and you will find general information about preparing your dog for show.

Shih Tzu Breed Standard

The Shih Tzu is a sturdy, lively, alert toy dog breed with flowing double coat that is accepted and recognized by the American Kennel Club (AKC). There are a lot of mix breeds or faults that are not accepted by the show people. Comply with these standards and you are good to go. This section will give you the breed standard and general guidelines on how to show your dog.

Official Shih Tzu Standard

General Appearance

Shih Tzus are only small breed with an ancient Chinese legacy. It is considered as highly valued, loyal companion, and a palace pet. Shih Tzus come in various size and shape; it still needs to comply with the standard set by the AKC.

Height and Weight

Ideally, Shih Tzus are typically 9 to 10 ½ inches tall, they can't be lower than 8 inches or taller than 11 inches. Adult Shih Tzus are around nine to 16 pounds. Keep this in mind when you want to show your Shih Tzus.

Head

- Its head is round and broad
- Wide space between eyes
- Head size is just proportional to its body.

Eyes and Eye Color

- Large, round, of equal distance
- Very dark eyes
- Liver and blue fur-colored dog have lighter-colored eye .

Skull and Muzzle

- The skull is domed.
- Has a stop
- The muzzle is square but not that prominent
- Unwrinkled but with great cushioning
- The front of the muzzle is flat; chin and lip are not protruding.

Expression

- Warm, sweet, wide-eyed, friendly, and trusting
- Has overall pleasant expressions.

Nose

- Should be black in color

Ears

- Large
- Heavily coated

Lips, Teeth and Bite

- Lips are tight fitting with the upper lip just covering the lower lip
- There is a strong lower jaw
- Should have black lips
- Broad and wide jaw
- There could be missing teeth and a misalignment of teeth
- Its teeth and tongue should be hidden when its mouth closed.

Neck and Chest

- Well set-on smoothly flowing into shoulders
- Great length for natural high head carriage
- Balanced weight and height
- The rib cage should be well sprung, must be oval in shape. Should have sufficient depth in order to reach the elbows.

Legs

- **Forequarters:** Shoulders: well laid-in, well laid-back, well-angulated, smoothly fit
- Legs - muscular, well-boned, straight
- Well-apart and under the chest
- Elbows are close to body
- Pasterns – Perpendicularly strong
- You may remove declaws.
- Well padded, pointing straight ahead, and firm feet

- **Hindquarters:** hindquarters must be well angulated and balanced with forequarters.
- Legs – straight, muscular, and wellboned when viewed from rear
- Far set but lined with forequarters.
- Hocks – perpendicular, let down
- Feet - Firm, well-padded, point straight ahead.

Feet

- **Front Feet:** Preferably rounded, close-cupped, well padded, and toes are well arched
- **Rear Feet:** Must be slightly toed out
- Must be rounded
- Forefeet should also be close-cupped
- Must have well-padded

- Toes should be well arched

Coat

- Flowing, luxurious, double coated, long, and dense
- Some waves are allowed.
- Tie the hair on head

Body Color and Markings

- Everything is permissible and accepted.

Gait

- The Shih Tzu walks straight
- At natural speed
- neither strung up or raced
- gently carried tail over its back.

Disqualifications

- **Head:** Narrow head, close-set eyes.
- **Eyes:** Small, close-set or light eyes; excessive eye white.
- **Muzzle:** Snipiness, lack of definite stop.
- Pink on nose, lips, or eye rims.
- Overshot bite

- Legginess
- Hyperextension of hocks
- Sparse coat, single coat, curly coat
- Excessive trimming

Preparing for the Show

After you have assessed your Shih Tzu, you can now enter it on a dog show. There are different dog shows year-round everywhere, you can check it on the AKC's website, or a Kennel Club within your area. Remember, look up all the rules and make extensive research to fully qualify for the show. Also, prepare your pup for the show.

Train your pup before entering the contest; create mock ups that would familiarize the dog with the set up in different competitions.

Here are some things you need to keep in mind while prepping your dog for show. These things are important as you need to keep your pups in the best quality as possible:

- Housetrain your pup before the show; you do not want to run around carrying poop bags during the show. Train your dog to have a specific area when it needs to go.

- Ensure that your dog is properly socialized to be in an environment with many other dogs and people. Introduce other dogs during play dates; also, you can introduce your friends to your dog as to see if your dog is ready to be introduced to more people at a larger venue. It may be scary at first, but you need to guide them step by step.

- Train your Shih Tzu to follow basic commands for obedience; this will be helpful during the show. This will ensure you that your Shih Tzus will follow you around and would not get lost; also, this will ensure that your dog will behave during the show.

- Research the requirements for the individual show and make sure your Shih Tzu meets them before you register. Prepare a list of things they need and bring the necessary documents when they need to see it.

- Take your Shih Tzu to its veterinarian frequently. Make sure to have its vaccine updated and free from any diseases. Ask your veterinarian for booster shots and tips on how to keep your Shih Tzus well behaved and healthy before, during, and after the show.

- Pack a bag of supplies for things that you and your Shih Tzu are likely to need at the show. Bring food, treats, and water for the show. You don't know how long your dog has to wait for its turn, you do not know how to starve your dog, but you do not want to keep it too full as it might feel sluggish and not perform well.

- Have your Shih Tzu groomed the week of the show and take steps to make sure his coat stays in good condition. Casually brush it every day to maintain its shininess.

Quick Checklist

Before you head on to your contest, make sure you have these things ready. It is best to prepare these things early on rather than forgetting on the day itself. Prepare a checklist of these things. Here are some things that may come in handy before, during and after the show:

- Registration information
- Dog crate or exercise pen
- Grooming table and grooming supplies
- Food and treats
- Food and water bowls
- Trash bags
- Medication (if needed)
- Change of clothes
- Food/water for self

- Paper towels or rags
- Toys for the dog

Chapter Eight: Breeding Your Shih Tzu

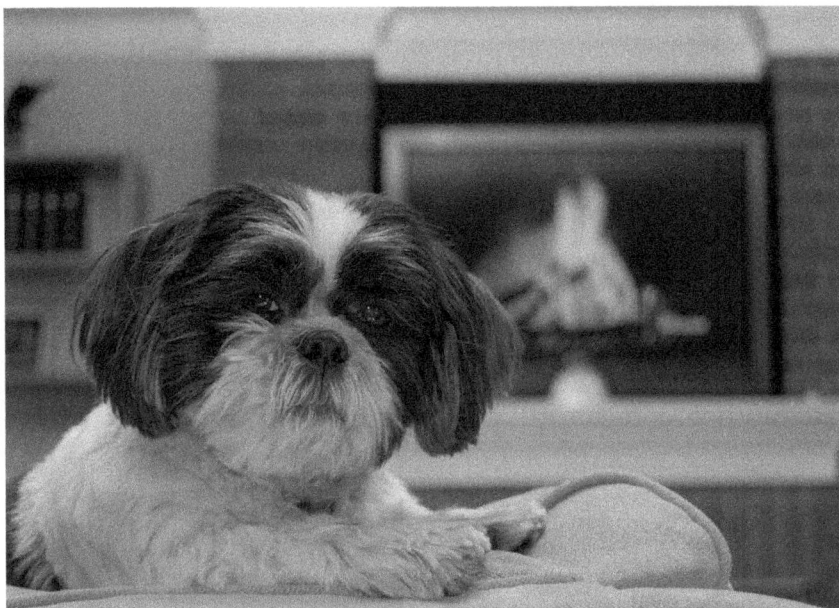

Buying two dogs at once, especially male and female dogs, is a big responsibility. You should keep in mind that there is a big possibility for breeding, especially if they stay in the same room together. You can build a happy Shih Tzu family and further develop a generation of this breed. Also, you could try to breed and sell these pups. Just take precaution as there are many things you would need during this process, also, this will require time, effort, and money.

You need to prepare yourself financially, emotionally, and physically. Some pups might not be able to make it out alive; you need to invest time into preparing both your male and female dog beforehand.

You need to give them the best nutrients and vitamins during its developmental years before you can start breeding it.

Here, we will give you detailed information on how to breed Shih Tzus properly. Further, we will give you the tips on how to raise your pups easily. Raising puppies are difficult, they are just like babies who need special needs especially during the first few days. Prepare your house, heart, and body for this tedious task. This task is not very easy, as you need to understand how to raise puppies, mother, and the adult Shih Tzu. But, you should always keep an open mind and read on if you want to try this endeavor.

Basic Dog Breeding Information

Breeding any type of dogs entails a big responsibility. You should decide carefully before you begin. Also, it can be a big financial problem if you are not prepared for breeding. You can start a big Shih Tzu family, give it to your family and friends, or even sell these for a small fortune..

Some dog owners think that dog breeding is an easy way to make extra money. However, there are costs that you need to look out for, such as prenatal vitamins, puppies, vitamins, and overall care. You will be very lucky if you make a small profit from your pups. It will drain you – but the process would be very rewarding, for you and your dogs.

If you do not plan to breed your Shih Tzu, you should have him or her neutered or spayed before 6 months of age. For female dogs, they should be spayed before their first heat. Keep in mind that spaying and neutering dogs before 6 months of age can significantly reduce their risk for certain types of cancer and other serious diseases.

If you do not want to spay or neuter your dog, make sure that your dog's stay in different rooms at all times. This act will prevent accidental mating.

Mating Behavior of Dogs

First thing you need to know about mating is the estrus cycle. This cycle is known as the "heat" period which female dogs experience twice a year. This cycle lasts for 14 to 21 days on average and it occurs about every 6 months once it becomes regular – it can take a few years for a dog to establish a regular cycle.

Your female dog might excrete a bloody discharge at the start of its cycle, or might not develop until the 7th day. This will be accompanied by the swelling of the vulva.

As the cycle progresses, the body discharge becomes lighter in color until it is pink and watery.

Further, female dogs might start urinate more than the usual, and might also develop urine marking behavior to attract the opposite gender.

A male dog can detect when a female is in heat from afar, you need to keep your female indoors when in heat. When in heat, make sure that your Shih Tzu is on a leash and closely supervise it especially during walks outside. Never let your female Shih Tzu in a dog park or any other location where there is a male dog present, especially if you want to breed your dog specifically for another dog.

A great sign for dog's fertility is when your dog's vulva becomes light in color and water, and then, she will ovulate – happens typically during days 11-15 of the cycle. This is a great time for you to introduce a male dog to your female dog. Don't introduce the dogs too early because your female may not be as receptive to the male. You can also try in a day or two after the first meeting. Shih Tzus are capable of conceiving at any point during her cycle, because the sperm can survive in the reproductive tract for as long as five days.

Tips for Breeding Your Shih Tzu

You have, now, made up your mind to breed your Shih Tzu. There are things you need to remember when breeding your Shih Tzu. It is more complicated than just having your dog's mate.

Here are some tips for you to remember when breeding your adult dogs. You need to follow these steps as they are vital to breeding them:

- **Study History:** Make sure you research the history of both the male and female dog. Make sure that both parties meet the AKC standards, so you can have a better breed, almost free on defects and flaws. Choose the best mate possible for your Shih Tzu.

- **Size:** Check to see that both male and female are proportionate in size and have pelvic breadth. Your female dog might struggle if you mate it with a bigger male dog.

- **Age:** The female dog must not be younger than eight months, while the male dog must not be less than seven months. In reality, the best age for a female dog to carry puppies is two years. Breeding dogs at an early age or at a late age will set on different deficiencies and possible health problems for the future pups.

- **Breeding goal:** If you own a female dog, make sure you know what you want, if you plan to breed small Shih Tzus or have different colored. This comes in handy especially when you study the history of both the male and female dog.

- **Don't overbreed:** You don't want to tire your female dog from too much breeding. You can mate it twice, and then allow it to rest. Also, you do not want to stress your female too much and resent to be bred anymore.

- **Think financially:** Breeding dogs is not a breeze, make sure you have enough budget set aside for vet consultations, vitamins, shots, deworming, and dog foods. Prepare your money beforehand and set up a trust fund for it.

- **Emotional preparation:** There are chances that some puppies won't make it out alive; you should be prepared for this loss.

- **Long-term commitment:** In some unfortunate incidence, you need to take care of the puppies that will be left by your side. Make sure they get sufficient care and love. You should have set a place where the puppies can grow and play.

Shih Tzu's Labor Process

Helping any dog give birth can be a stressful experience, but remember, it is still rewarding. Delivering puppies is very different from human's way. You can't just tell your female dog to 'push,' you need to guide it to ensure that every puppy will come out alive and healthy.

Your Shih Tzu due is around nine weeks. On the seventh and eighth week, you should prepare all the materials needed for delivery.

Prepare a quiet room within your home for the birthing process; this could help your Shih Tzu give birth easily. Since dogs have small pelvises, you need to watch out for signs of dog difficulties during birth.

Preparing for Birth

- You need to set up a box within your home. This will be a mini shelter for the pups and a place for the mother to bond with its litter.

- Place blankets all over the box, this will provide comfort for your Shih Tzu. Put a lamp near the box to provide heat for the puppies, but, make sure you place aluminum foil outside the lamp to prevent the accidents involving the puppies' eyes.

- Accustom the Shih Tzu in the box. Also, remove excess fur in the abdomen and underside area. This will help in the delivery and nursing activities.

- Take the temperature constantly. A drop in temperature is a sign for labor.

The Birthing Process

- Bring a laundry basket near the box; this basket will hold the newborn puppies. This will ensure that the mother could walk around until it has delivered all the puppies.

- Give your dog freedom to give birth on its own. You can remove the birthing sac from their faces only if the mother can't do it.

- Take a thread and tie it around the umbilical cord and tie another one an inch apart, then cut the cord between two threads.

- Let the mother lick the puppies' face, this will stimulate blood flow. If the mother can't do it, take the puppy and rub with a towel.

- Place the puppy in a towel inside the laundry basket.

- Let the mother and its puppy bond after birth. Give food and water after the process.

Chapter Nine: Keeping Your Shih Tzu Healthy

Taking care of dogs is such a big responsibility; it will not just stop from raising the puppies, you also need to know the health problems affecting your Shih Tzu.

You need to be aware of all the diseases and disorders that would cause future problems for your pet. The knowledge on this matter could help you big time. You need to keep an open eye on all the possibilities for these diseases. Keep an open eye for signs and symptoms as to easily prevent them.

Watch Out for this Illnesses

Here, we will give you lots of information that may affect your Shih Tzu's health. Learning these things will arm you with basic knowledge on all the possibilities. Know the causes, signs, symptoms, and remedies so you can be ready in any situation.

As for your Shih Tzu, you need to take special care for ears, eyes, nose, and mouth. These parts are easily susceptible for sickness and are prone to infection. Further, Shih Tzus are indoor dogs, so you shouldn't let them out for too long, especially during summer.

Eye Diseases

- **Dry Eyes** – this occurs when a dog has insufficient tears to keep its eye lubricated. This will result in mucoid discharge that will stay in one's eye. Normally, you will see a big "gunk" around its eyes, and the eyelid rubs the cornea making it very cloudy.

- **Cherry Eyes** – this happens when there is a prolapse in the dog's third eyelid. There is a development of red mass on the corner of the affected eye.

- **Juvenile Cataract** – this usually happens on older dogs or to dogs who are suffering from diabetes. Your dog would have 'clouding' in its lens.

- **Entropion** – this has a gooey eye discharge that would lead to more serious problem like glaucoma, cataract, or corneal ulceration.

Face Diseases/Problems

- **Brachycephalic Syndrome** – Simply put it, this disease obstructs the airway of your puppy, and this will cause noisy breathing, coughing and gagging, fainting, collapsing episodes or even a decrease in tolerance for exercises.

- **Cleft Lip/Palate** – this happens when the opening of the lip or even the roof of the mouth didn't process normally during its conception.

Other Diseases

- **Patellar Luxation** – commonly known as arthritis, this disease could even affect young dogs. It is a painful disease that will affect the dog's comfort, lifestyle, and even emotional wellbeing.

- **Hip Dysplasia** – one common form of arthritis, this refers to an abnormality in growth and development of the ball and socket on the dog's hips.

- **Renal Dysplasia** – this affects puppies and young dogs, it is a very serious developmental disorder affecting its kidneys. This could sometimes happen when the kidneys are underdeveloped.

Recommended Vaccinations

Just like newborn babies, puppies need to be vaccinated. This happens because newborn puppies are not really immune to several diseases.

If the mother has contracted the disease already, the mother would send the antibodies through the placenta; this will ensure that the puppies would receive more protection especially when they drink the first milk. The first milk, also called the colostrum, is excreted by the mother after 36 to 48 hours after its birth. Make sure that the pups have drunk this, because it is rich in antibiotics provided by the mother.

The Need for Vaccination

The maternal antibodies given by the mother to its puppies will protect from several diseases. But, these antibodies would not stay forever; a good way to keep your puppy healthy is through vaccination.

Types of Vaccines

Puppy vaccines are just like any vaccines that contain antigens, which have three types:

- **Modified Live Vaccines (MLV)** – contains a weak strain of the disease that would replicate once in a dog, but would not really harm it.

- **Inactivated or Killed Vaccine** – contains the killed whole agent. Oldest and the most trusted vaccine, because it has the longest shelf life.

- **Recombinant Technology** – contains the freshest and best results possible. This has the most advanced vaccine.

The Needed Vaccines

These vaccines should not only be given to Shih Tzu puppies but for all kinds of dogs. They help the dogs in combatting diseases:

- **Parvovirus** – a highly contagious virus that would involve vomiting, diarrhea, depression, and lethargy.

- **Distemper** – includes coughing, sneezing, fever, and loss of appetite. This could infect other dogs through bodily secretions.

- **Canine Hepatitis** – affects liver and can potentially lead to death.

With these in mind, you should decide to have your puppies vaccinated as soon as possible.

Vaccination Tips

- Ask your vet on the best age before subjecting your puppy to vaccination
- Get your puppies booster shots for common diseases

- The first shot should be given during six to eight weeks. This will be followed up until it has completed four rounds.
- Rabies vaccination will be given to 16 to 26 week old puppies, then once a year.
- Remember to keep their vaccines, booster, and rabies shot updated as to protect them to different diseases.

Chapter Ten: Shih Tzu Checklist and Summary

You have gone through a lot when you have read this book, now, it is time for you to buy your puppy and apply these things in real life! You can search up for more information through other books or websites for further knowledge. This will enable you to become the best breeder with happy and healthy puppies. This last part will give you the overview of our beloved furry friend. Take note of these things as they might come handy someday.

Quick Checklist of Shih Tzu

Basic Information

- o **Pedigree**: Shih Tzu
- o **AKC Group**: Toy group
- o **Breed Size**: Small
- o **Height:** 11 inches or 27.94 cm
- o **Weight:** average of 9 – 16 pounds
- o **Coat Length**: dense, long, and flowing double coat
- o **Coat Texture**: soft, puffy
- o **Color**: black, white, brindle, liver, blue, liver & white, black & white, light brown, dark brown, and gold
- o **Temperament**: fierce, well-behaved, alert, vigilant, affectionate, courageous, friendly
- o **Strangers**: friendly around strangers
- o **Other Dogs**: both genders get along with other dogs
- o **Other Pets**: gets along well with other pets
- o **Training**: needs firm but gentle leadership
- o **Exercise Needs**: very little
- o **Health Conditions**: generally healthy, but to susceptible to diseases relating to eye, ear, mouth, and body.
- o **Lifespan**: average 10 to 16 years

Habitat Requirements

- o **Recommended Accessories**: crate, dog bed, food/water dishes, toys, collar, leash, harness, grooming supplies
- o **Collar and Harness**: sized by weight
- o **Grooming Supplies**: soft brittle brush, nail clipper, dematting comb
- o **Grooming Frequency**: occasional, need to detangle fur
- o **Energy Level**: somehow active and alert
- o **Exercise Requirements**: frequent exercises is needed
- o **Crate**: not that much recommended
- o **Crate Size**: small to medium sized
- o **Food/Water**: preferably stainless steel or ceramic bowls
- o **Toys**: start with an assortment, see what the dog likes; include some mentally stimulating toys
- o **Training**: responds well

Nutritional Needs

- o **Nutritional Needs**: water, protein, carbohydrate, fats, vitamins, minerals
- o **Calorie Needs**: varies by age, weight, and activity level; RER modified with activity level

- Amount to Feed (puppy): feed freely but consult recommendations on the package preferably 3 – 6 times a day.
- Amount to Feed (adult): consult recommendations on the package; calculated by weight
- Important Ingredients: fresh animal protein (chicken, beef, lamb, turkey, eggs), digestible carbohydrates (rice, oats, barley), animal fats
- Important Minerals: calcium, phosphorus, potassium, magnesium, iron, copper and manganese
- Important Vitamins: Vitamin A, Vitamin A, Vitamin B-12, Vitamin D, Vitamin C
- Certifications: AAFCO statement of nutritional adequacy; protein at top of ingredients list; no artificial flavors, dyes, preservatives

Breeding Information

- Age of First Heat: around 6 or 7 months (or earlier)
- Heat (Estrus) Cycle: 15 to 21 days
- Frequency: once or twice a year
- Greatest Fertility: 11 to 15 days into the cycle
- Gestation Period: 59 to 63 days
- Pregnancy Detection: possible after 24 to 25 days, best to wait 45 days for the ultrasound
- Feeding Pregnant Dogs: maintain normal diet until week 5 or 6 then slightly increase rations

- o **Signs of Labor**: body temperature drops below normal 100° to 102°F (37.7° to 38.8°C), may be as low as 98°F (36.6°C); dog begins nesting in a dark, quiet place
- o **Contractions**: period of 10 minutes in waves of 2 to 3 followed by a period of rest
- o **Whelping**: puppies are born in 1/2 hour increments following 10 to 30 minutes of forceful straining
- o **Puppies**: born with eyes and ears closed; eyes open at 3 weeks, teeth develop at 10 weeks
- o **Litter Size**: average 6 to 12 puppies
- o **Size at Birth**: about 100 pounds or more
- o **Weaning**: start offering puppy food soaked in water at 6 weeks; fully weaned by 8 weeks
- o **Socialization**: start as early as possible to prevent puppies from being nervous as an adult

Summary

History/Origin:

- This breed was believed to be a crossbreed between small Tibetan dog breeds, such as Lhasa Apsos and Pekingese.

- Many people have associated the breed with Dowager Empress Tzu His, who ruled China in 1861-1908, and labeled the dogs as sacred

- They were believed to have carried lamas souls who had not yet reached nirvana.

- Traditionally called "Shih-tzu Kou" or "Lion Dog"

Nicknames for Shih Tzus:

- Chin Chia Huang Pao – golden yellow dog
- Chin Pan To Yueh – yellow dog with white mane
- Yi Ting Mo – black dogs
- Hua Tse – multicolored dog

What Makes It a Great Pet:

- A Shih Tzu is an excellent choice if you want a lovable housedog as a companion
- Shih Tzus are known as loyal and devoted dogs especially to their masters.
- They are only a small breed which is great for apartments and small homes
- They only require short walks or an indoor play time.
- They can easily adapt to new environments. They can be introduced to new people and pets.

Obtaining a Pet License:

- **U.S.:** You will have to provide proof that your dog has been vaccinated against rabies.
- **UK:** Dog licenses are renewed annually; no need for a vaccination proof

Costs for Keeping:

- Shih Tzu Price: ranges from $700 to $2,000
- Bed ($10-$50)
- Toys ($20-$100)
- Grooming Tools ($100-$500)
- Dog Food and Treats ($50-100)
- Vet Consultations: starts at $40
- Micro-chipping: $50
- Initial Vaccinations: starts at $50
- Spay/Neuter Surgery: $50 - $175

Where to Purchase?

Local Pet Stores:

Pros:

- Accessible
- Can be delivered to your house

Cons:

- Insufficient information of how the pet was bred.
- May not be of the best quality

Backyard/Private Breeders

Pros:

- Considered as the best option when purchasing dog breeds
- The breed is of great quality almost all the time
- An opportunity to bargain for a lower price
- This path is best for sociable people who want to meet new breeders.

Cons:

- You need to come to the house/place personally to visit and inspect the puppies
- Not for those who does not have time to talk to people and investigate on their background.

Online Stores

Pros:

- This will be a great option if you are a busy person
- You can join online forums to know which sites would give you the best breed possible

Cons:

- You won't have the opportunity to critique how the pup was bred, its health, and its parent.
- You need to keep a keen eye on its physical characteristics before buying it

Reminders When Looking for the Best Shih Tzu:

- Examine the pup's body thoroughly for any signs of illness and potential injuries.
- The pup/s should be active, and playful, interacting with each other in a healthy way.
- If all the pups are in good condition, and seems to like you, that's a good sign that your breeder is also reputable.
- Choose who best connects with you.

Tips in Puppy Proofing

- Remove any toxic houseplants from your home or move your plants so they are well out of your puppy's reach.
- Cover any open bodies of water that could pose a drowning hazard for your puppy – this includes toilets, sinks, ponds, pools, and more.
- You need to have toys and chew toys while you are away. Some pups might misbehave when you are not

around, to prevent this from happening, they should have leisure activities in their area.

- Secure all your appliances; tie up the cords for your blinds as well as electric cords so your puppy can't chew on them.

Recommended Food Brands for Shih Tzus:

- **Royal Canin Shih Tzu Dog Food:** This food has kibbles that make it easy for your Shih Tzu to eat
- **EUKANUBA:** This dog food is a runner up as the best dog food for your Shih Tzu. It's also good for Yorkshire Terriers if you have one.
- **Wellness CORE Natural Grain Free Dry Dog Food:** It is grain free that has balanced everyday nutrition for your beloved pup; this is packed with calories so you can be assured that your Shih Tzu has high energy levels.

Tips on Choosing the Best Brand:

<u>**Get to know your dog**</u>

- Puppies and mother need more calories as they need more energy due to high activity.
- Older dogs need fewer calories because they don't move much.
- Active dogs need more food than lap dogs.

Read the food packaging

- Dinner dog foods only contain 25% of the protein it needs.
- Cheese-based dog food would only contain 3% of the actual nutrient.

Learn the Ingredients

- Choose the brand which lists meat first because it contains the highest water content for it.

Go easy on switching diets

- Switching their diet to grains is not really a bad idea, but, it has a higher price point so you need to be prepared.

Know the nutritional adequacy

- A good way to know the nutritional adequacy is looking at the Association of American Feed Control Officials (AAFCO)'s standard

Research and list down the pros and cons

- Research on the manufacturers, quality control, and sourcing of ingredients.

Grooming Needs:

- Bath
- Removing mat
- Check anal glands
- Spritz cologne
- Clean ears
- Cut dog's hair
- Clip nails

Tools for Grooming:

- Straight shears
- Curve shears
- Thinning or blending scissors
- Blunt tipped scissors
- Dematting combs
- Blow dryer
- Shampoo and conditioner
- Nail clippers
- Dog-friendly ear cleaning solution
- Dog toothbrush
- Dog-friendly toothpaste

Showing Your Shih Tzu Tips:

- Housetrain your pup before the show
- Ensure that your dog is properly socialized
- Train your Shih Tzu to follow basic commands for obedience
- Research the requirements for the individual show
- Take your Shih Tzu to its veterinarian frequently
- Bring food, treats, and water for the show.
- Casually brush your dog's coat every day to maintain its shininess.

Tips for Breeding Your Shih Tzu

- Make sure you research the history of both the male and female dog.
- Check to see that both male and female are proportionate in size and have pelvic breadth.
- The female dog must not be younger than eight months, while the male dog must not be less than seven months.
- Have a breeding goal
- Don't overbreed
- Think financially
- Be emotionally prepare
- Be ready for a long-term commitment

Common Illness of Shih Tzus:

- Dry Eyes
- Cherry Eyes
- Juvenile Cataract
- Entropion
- Brachycephalic Syndrome
- Cleft Lip/Palate
- Patellar Luxation
- Hip Dysplasia
- Renal Dysplasia

Types of Dog Vaccines:

- Modified Live Vaccines (MLV)
- Inactivated or Killed Vaccine
- Recombinant Technology

Recommended Vaccines for Shih Tzus:

- Parvovirus
- Distemper
- Canine Hepatitis

Glossary of Pup Terms

Abundism – Referring to a pup that has markings more prolific than is normal.

Acariasis – A type of mite infection.

ACF – Australian Pup Federation

Affix – A puptery name that follows the pup's registered name; puptery owner, not the breeder of the pup.

Agouti – A type of natural coloring pattern in which individual hairs have bands of light and dark coloring.

Ailurophile – A person who loves pups.

Albino – A type of genetic mutation which results in little to no pigmentation, in the eyes, skin, and coat.

Allbreed – Referring to a show that accepts all breeds or a judge who is qualified to judge all breeds.

Alley Pup – A non-pedigreed pup.

Alter – A desexed pup; a male pup that has been neutered or a female that has been spayed.

Amino Acid – The building blocks of protein; there are 22 types for pups, 11 of which can be synthesized and 11 which must come from the diet (see essential amino acid).

Anestrus – The period between estrus cycles in a female pup.

Any Other Variety (AOV) – A registered pup that doesn't conform to the breed standard.

ASH – American Shorthair, a breed of pup.

Back Cross – A type of breeding in which the offspring is mated back to the parent.

Balance – Referring to the pup's structure; proportional in accordance with the breed standard.

Barring – Describing the tabby's striped markings.

Base Color – The color of the coat.

Bicolor – A pup with patched color and white.

Blaze – A white coloring on the face, usually in the shape of an inverted V.

Bloodline – The pedigree of the pup.

Brindle – A type of coloring, a brownish or tawny coat with streaks of another color.

Castration – The surgical removal of a male pup's testicles.

Pup Show – An event where pups are shown and judged.

Puptery – A registered pup breeder; also, a place where pups may be boarded.

CFA – The Pup Fanciers Association.

Cobby – A compact body type.

Colony – A group of pups living wild outside.

Color Point – A type of coat pattern that is controlled by color point alleles; pigmentation on the tail, legs, face, and ears with an ivory or white coat.

Colostrum – The first milk produced by a lactating female; contains vital nutrients and antibodies.

Conformation – The degree to which a pedigreed pup adheres to the breed standard.

Cross Breed – The offspring produced by mating two distinct breeds.

Dam – The female parent.

Declawing – The surgical removal of the pup's claw and first toe joint.

Developed Breed – A breed that was developed through selective breeding and crossing with established breeds.

Down Hairs – The short, fine hairs closest to the body which keep the pup warm.

DSH – Domestic Shorthair.

Estrus – The reproductive cycle in female pups during which she becomes fertile and receptive to mating.

Fading Pup Syndrome – Pups that die within the first two weeks after birth; the cause is generally unknown.

Feral – A wild, untamed pup of domestic descent.

Gestation – Pregnancy; the period during which the fetuses develop in the female's uterus.

Guard Hairs – Coarse, outer hairs on the coat.

Harlequin – A type of coloring in which there are van markings of any color with the addition of small patches of the same color on the legs and body.

Inbreeding – The breeding of related pups within a closed group or breed.

Kibble – Another name for dry pup food.

Lilac – A type of coat color that is pale pinkish-gray.

Line – The pedigree of ancestors; family tree.

Litter – The name given to a group of pups born at the same time from a single female.

Mask – A type of coloring seen on the face in some breeds.

Matts – Knots or tangles in the pup's fur.

Mittens – White markings on the feet of a pup.

Moggie – Another name for a mixed breed pup.

Mutation – A change in the DNA of a cell.

Muzzle – The nose and jaws of an animal.

Natural Breed – A breed that developed without selective breeding or the assistance of humans.

Neutering – Desexing a male pup.

Open Show – A show in which spectators are allowed to view the judging.

Pads – The thick skin on the bottom of the feet.

Particolor – A type of coloration in which there are markings of two or more distinct colors.

Patched – A type of coloration in which there is any solid color, tabby, or tortoiseshell color plus white.

Pedigree – A purebred pup; the pup's papers showing its family history.

Pet Quality – A pup that is not deemed of high enough standard to be shown or bred.

Piebald – A pup with white patches of fur.

Points – Also color points; markings of contrasting color on the face, ears, legs, and tail.

Pricked – Referring to ears that sit upright.

Purebred – A pedigreed pup.

Queen – An intact female pup.

Roman Nose – A type of nose shape with a bump or arch.

Scruff – The loose skin on the back of a pup's neck.

Selective Breeding – A method of modifying or improving a breed by choosing pups with desirable traits.

Senior – A pup that is more than 5 but less than 7 years old.

Sire – The male parent of a pup.

Solid – Also self; a pup with a single coat color.

Spay – Desexing a female pup.

Stud – An intact male pup.

Tabby – A type of coat pattern consisting of a contrasting color over a ground color.

Tom Pup – An intact male pup.

Tortoiseshell – A type of coat pattern consisting of a mosaic of red or cream and another base color.

Tri-Color – A type of coat pattern consisting of three distinct colors in the coat.

Tuxedo – A black and white pup.

Unaltered – A pup that has not been desexed.

Index

H

I

J

K

L

S

T

U

V

W

Photo Credits

Page 1 Photo by user Robyn Randell via Pixabay.com, https://pixabay.com/en/dog-shih-tzu-white-grey-cute-1193114/

Page 4 Photo by user wernerdetjen via Pixabay.com, https://pixabay.com/en/animal-portrait-puppy-dog-shih-tzu-2499092/

Page 10 Photo by user cesar_abud via Pixabay.com, https://pixabay.com/en/pet-shih-tzu-dog-puppy-2530265/

Page 24 Photo by user Jai79 via Pixabay.com, https://pixabay.com/en/dog-puppy-shih-tzu-tibetan-terrier-2746234/

Page 40 Photo by user tookapic via Pixabay.com, https://pixabay.com/en/dog-backyard-canine-pet-animal-932447/

Page 48 Photo by user cesar_abud via Pixabay.com, https://pixabay.com/en/pet-shih-tzu-dog-puppy-2530262/

Page 60 Photo by user 12122 via Pixabay.com, https://pixabay.com/en/dog-shih-tzu-animal-small-fluffy-64327/

Page 70 Photo by user carlosleucipo via Pixabay.com, https://pixabay.com/en/shih-tzu-animal-dog-grass-hairy-1794595/

Page 80 Photo by user mintchipdesigns via Pixabay.com, https://pixabay.com/en/shih-tzu-dog-pet-animal-canine-499390/

Page 90 Photo by user carlosleucipo via Pixabay.com, https://pixabay.com/en/shih-tzu-animal-ball-grass-dog-1794593/

Page 97 Photo by user Kaz via Pixabay.com, https://pixabay.com/en/dog-shih-tzu-cute-animal-pet-164190/

References

"6 Steps to Choosing The Best Food For Your Dog"
Barkpost.com
https://stories.barkpost.com/best-dog-food/

"Bathing a Shih Tzu" Allshihtzu.com
http://www.allshihtzu.com/bathing-a-shih-tzu

"Breeding Tips" Allshihtzu.com
http://www.allshihtzu.com/breeding-a-shih-tzu

"Cherry Eye in Dogs" Natural-dog-health-remedies.com
https://www.natural-dog-health-remedies.com/cherry-eye-in-dogs.html

"Dog Nutrition Tips" ASPCA.org
https://www.aspca.org/pet-care/dog-care/dog-nutrition-tips

"Dry Eye in Dogs" Natural-dog-health-remedies.com
https://www.natural-dog-health-remedies.com/dry-eye-in-dogs.html

"Feeding Information of a Shih Tzu" Petsworld.in
https://www.petsworld.in/blog/shih-tzu-feeding-tips.html

"Grooming the Shih Tzu" Miracleshihtzu.com
https://www.miracleshihtzu.com/grooming-the-shih-tzu.html

"Grooming Supplies Checklist" Miracleshihtzu.com
https://www.miracleshihtzu.com/shih-tzu-grooming-supplies.html

"Grooming Tools for a Shih Tzu" Allshihtzu.com
http://www.allshihtzu.com/shih-tzu-grooming-tools

"How to Clip Dog Nails" Miracleshihtzu.com
https://www.miracleshihtzu.com/how-to-clip-dog-nails.html

"How to Help a Shih Tzu Give Birth" Cuteness.com
https://www.cuteness.com/article/shih-tzu-give-birth

"How Much Food Does Your Shih Tzu Puppy Need?"
Shihtzuwire.com
http://shihtzuwire.com/much-food-shih-tzu-puppy-need/

"My Dog Won't Eat"- What To Do With a Picky Eater?" DrHarveys.com
https://www.drharveys.com/blog/post/34-my-dog-won-t-eat-what-to-do-with-a-picky-eater

"Shih Tzu" Vetstreet.com
http://www.vetstreet.com/dogs/shih-tzu

"Shih Tzu" AKC.org
http://www.akc.org/dog-breeds/shih-tzu/

"Shih Tzu Brushes" Miracleshihtzu.com
(What's in Your Grooming Bag?)
https://www.miracleshihtzu.com/shih-tzu-brushes.html

"Shih Tzu Health Problems" Natural-dog-health-remedies.com
https://www.natural-dog-health-remedies.com/shih-tzu-health-problems.html

"The Benefits and Drawbacks of Owning a Shih Tzu" Shihtzuwire.com
http://shihtzuwire.com/benefits-drawbacks-owning-shih-tzu/

"What vaccines does your dog really need?"
Shihtzusbyelaine.com
http://www.shihtzusbyelaine.com/vaccine-recommedations-
-contagious-diseases.html

"Vaccinating Your Shih Tzu" HealthGuidance.org
http://www.healthguidance.org/entry/6896/1/Vaccinating-
Your-Shih-Tzu.html

"Your Dog's Nutritional Needs" Nas.edu
http://dels.nas.edu/resources/static-
assets/banr/miscellaneous/dog_nutrition_final_fix.pdf

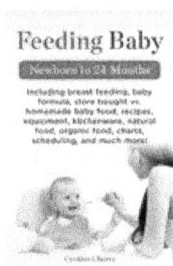

Feeding Baby
Cynthia Cherry
978-1941070000

Axolotl
Lolly Brown
978-0989658430

Dysautonomia, POTS
Syndrome
Frederick Earlstein
978-0989658485

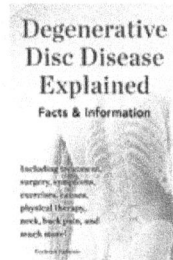

Degenerative Disc
Disease Explained
Frederick Earlstein
978-0989658485

Sinusitis, Hay Fever,
Allergic Rhinitis Explained
Frederick Earlstein
978-1941070024

Wicca
Riley Star
978-1941070130

Zombie Apocalypse
Rex Cutty
978-1941070154

Capybara
Lolly Brown
978-1941070062

Eels As Pets
Lolly Brown
978-1941070167

Scabies and Lice Explained
Frederick Earlstein
978-1941070017

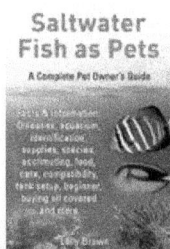

Saltwater Fish As Pets
Lolly Brown
978-0989658461

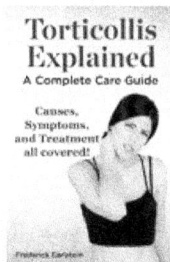

Torticollis Explained
Frederick Earlstein
978-1941070055

Kennel Cough
Lolly Brown
978-0989658409

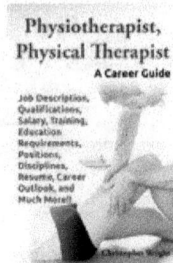

Physiotherapist, Physical
Therapist
Christopher Wright
978-0989658492

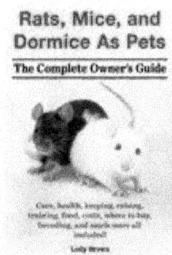

Rats, Mice, and Dormice
As Pets
Lolly Brown
978-1941070079

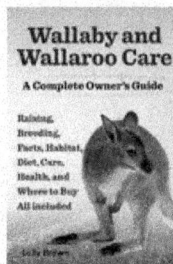

Wallaby and Wallaroo Care
Lolly Brown
978-1941070031

Bodybuilding Supplements
Explained
Jon Shelton
978-1941070239

Demonology
Riley Star
978-19401070314

Pigeon Racing
Lolly Brown
978-1941070307

Dwarf Hamster
Lolly Brown
978-1941070390

Cryptozoology
Rex Cutty
978-1941070406

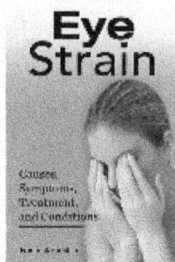

Eye Strain
Frederick Earlstein
978-1941070369

Inez The Miniature Elephant
Asher Ray
978-1941070353

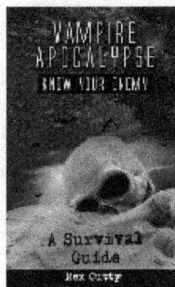

Vampire Apocalypse
Rex Cutty
978-1941070321